M000211401

**? Essential Question**
How are families around the world
the same and different?

# Music in My Family

by Parker Wu
illustrated by Ethan Long

Myra is going to a music festival. She is going with her father. Her friend Lucy is coming, too.

"What will we see?"
asks Myra.

"We will see many bands,"
Dad says. "People from
around the world have
been invited to play.
They will sing in different
languages."

Myra and Lucy love music. Their families do, too.

"My mom plays the guitar," Myra says.

"My dad plays the piano," Lucy says.

Dad and the girls arrive
at the festival. Dad says,
"I have a surprise for you!
But you will have to wait."

"That's not fair. Tell us
now," the girls plead. But
Dad just smiles.

5

The girls look around. A band is playing. People are having picnics. They share food.

"I like the drums!" Lucy says.

"I like the flute!" says Myra.

Dad takes the girls aside. "That band is from India," he says.

"Look! His hand scurries up and down so fast!" says Lucy.

Dad says, "This band is from Africa."

"That instrument sounds like a bird," says Myra.

Dad says, "That band is from Australia."

"Those low notes sound like the wind," says Lucy.

A new band is starting.

"Time for the surprise!"
grins Dad.

The band walks onto
the stage.

"That's Mom!" cries Myra.

Mom plays her guitar. She sings in Spanish.

Myra is smiling. They all
feel so proud!

# Respond to Reading

## Summarize

Use details to help you summarize *Music in My Family*.

| Character | Setting | Events |
|-----------|---------|--------|
|           |         |        |
|           |         |        |

## Text Evidence

1. How do you know *Music in My Family* is realistic fiction? Genre

2. Who are the characters in the story? Use story details. Character, Setting, Events

3. Use what you know about root words to figure out what *playing* means on page 6. Root Words

4. Write about what Myra learns at the festival. Write About Reading

**Compare Texts**

Read about some of the different ways that people make music.

# Making Music

The sitar is a popular musical instrument in Indian culture. It has seventeen strings. Its body is pear-shaped.

India

17

The mbira has a wooden board and metal keys. Players pluck the keys.

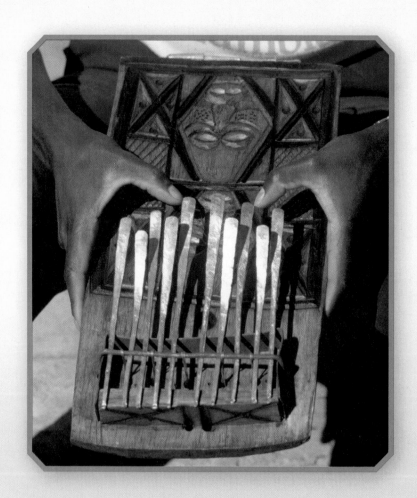

Australia

The didgeridoo is a long tube. It is made from a hollow branch.

## Make Connections

How do people around the world make music? **Essential Question**

How is a sitar like a guitar?

Text to Text

# Focus on
# Social Studies

**Purpose** To compare ways we celebrate special times

## What to Do

**Step 1** Work with a partner. Think of something you celebrate with your family, like a holiday or birthday.

**Step 2** Draw a picture of how you celebrate. Share your picture with your partner.

**Step 3** Talk about how you both celebrate special times.